GROW Crystal Jewelry

by the editors of Klutz

KLUTZ

IMPORTANT SAFETY INFORMATION

- **This kit is only for use by children over 8 years of age.** Not for use by children under 8 years of age. Store this kit out of reach of young children, and keep young children and pets away from experiments and supplies.
- This kit is to be used solely under the strict supervision of adults who have studied the precautions and instructions in the book and packaging.
- Read the instructions before use, follow them, and keep them for reference. Save packaging and instructions as they contain important information.
- Read and follow these instructions, the safety rules, and the first aid information, and keep them for reference. The incorrect use of chemicals can cause injury and damage to health. Only carry out those activities which are listed in the instructions.
- The area surrounding the activity should be kept clear of any obstructions and away from the storage of food. It should be well lit, well ventilated, and close to a water supply. A solid table with a heat-resistant top should be provided.

Please note the following risk and safety information for the substances contained in this kit:

- The crystal powder (aluminum potassium sulfate) can cause irritation to your eyes, mouth, and skin. Avoid skin contact with the dry powder or liquid solution.
- The dye tablets can stain. Avoid skin contact and protect fabrics and surfaces. The yellow dye contains Yellow #5 which is a known irritant for people with certain sensitivities and allergies.
- Eye protection is not included, but is recommended for additional safety precaution.

Advice for parents and supervising adults:

- The activities in this book have been designed for children ages 8 and up. However, since children's abilities vary so much, even within age groups, you should review the instructions first and exercise discretion as to which experiments are suitable and safe for them.
- The substances and components in this kit have been tested to U.S., Canada, and Australia/New Zealand safety standards. Per these standards, there are no dangerous chemicals included in this kit. However, it is recommended that adults assist in all activities as misuse could result in injury.
- Before starting the experiments, your child should carefully read through all the instructions and warnings, and you should discuss the warnings and safety information with your child to make sure they fully understand them. Emphasize to your child the importance of following all instructions and warnings, and the importance of carrying out only those experiments that are described in this book.

First aid information:

- **Important:** In case of injury, always seek medical help. Bring the chemical and its packaging with you.
- **To contact your local Poison Control Center, please dial:**
  - United States: 1-800-222-1222
  - Canada: 1-416-813-5900
  - New Zealand: 0800 764 766
  - Australia: 13 11 26
- **In case of eye contact:** Wash out eye with plenty of water, holding the eye open if necessary. Seek immediate medical help.
- **If swallowed:** Do not induce vomiting. Seek immediate medical advice.
- For any injuries or adverse reactions, seek medical advice.

CONTENTS

What You Get 4
A Note on Safety 6
Setting Up Your Lab 8
Crystal Science 10
Crystals vs. Gems 14

Color Notes 21
Finishing Your Jewelry 22

Making Solutions 16
    Seeding Solution 16
    Growing Solution 18

Projects 25
    Crystal Stick Pendant 26
    Wire Coil Earrings 30
    Crystal Ring 32
    Geode Slice Pendant 36
    Zigzag Pendant 40
    Colossal Crystal 43
Troubleshooting 47

WHAT YOU GET

CRYSTAL POWDER: You get enough crystal powder to make seven projects, depending on the size of the crystals that you grow. Flip through the book and choose your favorites—make these projects first.

GLAZE: Once you've grown your crystals, you'll glaze them to brighten their colors (page 23).

NECKLACE CORD

CRAFT STICKS

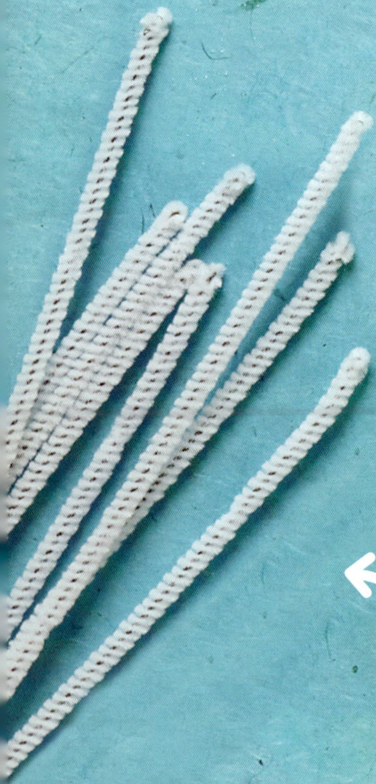

PIPE CLEANERS: Pipe cleaners will be the base for most of your jewelry. Snip off the ends before you start.

JEWELRY FINDINGS:
You'll use lobster clasps, cord ends, jump rings, earring wires, ring blanks, and jewelry wire to make your crystal creations wearable. Turn to pages 23–24 to learn how to build your jewelry.

LOBSTER CLASPS

JUMP RINGS

CORD ENDS

NYLON THREAD

GOLD WIRE

EARRING WIRES

RING BLANKS

OTHER STUFF YOU'LL NEED

- ▶ Small, heatproof jars with lids, about 10 fl oz (296 mL)
- ▶ Liquid measuring cup and tablespoons
- ▶ Small pot
- ▶ Distilled water
- ▶ Long-handled metal spoon (for crafting only)
- ▶ Masking tape
- ▶ Pencil or marker
- ▶ High-quality clear nail polish

LOOSE GLITTER

DYE TABLETS: You'll use these dye tablets to color your crystals. To learn how to dye your jewels and to mix custom colors, turn to page 21.

A NOTE ON SAFETY

Editors' note: Here at Klutz Galactic HQ, we want you to be safe *and* have fun, so read this before you start crystallizing.

GENERAL TIPS

▶ Adult supervision is required for your experiments. Supervising adults should also read the instructions in the book before starting any experiment.

▶ Read the instructions before you start, follow them, and keep them handy so you can look things up when you need to. Only stick to the experiments and crafts recommended in this book.

▶ The projects in this book are for readers 8 years old and up. Keep your experiments away from young children and pets, and store your supplies and jewelry where young children and pets can't reach them.

WORKING WITH CRYSTAL POWDER & SOLUTIONS

▶ Perform experiments in areas away from food and drinks and bedrooms. Don't use jars or utensils from your crystal experiments to store or prepare food or drinks afterward. Don't use drinking glasses—only heat-resistant jars.

▶ To open the crystal powder packet, cut along the dotted line at the top with scissors. Make sure you cut above the resealable lock on the bag. Don't use your teeth to open the packet!

▶ Keep the crystal powder, growing solution, and crystals away from your eyes, nose, and mouth.

▶ Don't let crystal powder or growing solution come into contact with the skin. If powder or growing solution does come in contact with your skin, clean the area with soap and water.

▶ To dispose of crystals, throw solid crystals and powders in the trash. Pour liquid solution directly into the sink drain.

HANDLING HOT STUFF

▶ Only adults should heat liquids and handle hot jars and utensils. Do not leave the stove unattended while heating water or growing solution. Remember to turn off stove burners when you're done using them.

▶ When reheating growing solution, leave the jar open. Never use a microwave to heat water, seeding solution, or growing solution.

▶ Use a potholder or kitchen towel to handle hot jars. Always place hot jars on a trivet or potholder to cool.

▶ Let hot jars cool slowly at room temperature. Do not put jars in the refrigerator or in the freezer to cool them.

▶ Remember: Steam is very hot! Avoid contact with steam since it may cause burns. Also avoid inhaling any steam or vapors from hot growing solution.

DYE TABLETS

▶ Be careful when using dye tablets since they may cause stains that won't wash out of fabrics.

▶ Perform experiments away from furniture and carpets that you don't want to accidentally stain.

WEARING JEWELRY

▶ Only wear crystals as jewelry once they've been coated with glaze and dried completely.

▶ When painting with glaze, work near an open window or door for ventilation. Avoid breathing in the vapors from the glaze.

▶ If you develop a rash while wearing your crystal jewelry, take it off right away. See a doctor if the rash doesn't go away after a few days.

SETTING UP YOUR LAB

LAB REQUIREMENTS

A FLAT WORK SURFACE: The best place is a solid table that's heat resistant, which means that it's OK to place hot things on it. You'll also want your work surface to be out of reach of any nosy siblings or pets and away from food or drinks.

NOT TOO HOT: The best place for your lab is somewhere where there's a constant temperature, so pick a place away from sunny windows.

PREVENT MESSES: In case of spills, put down some newspaper or paper towels before you start your experiments. For hot jars, be sure to put down a trivet or a potholder first to protect your work surface.

YOUR UNIFORM: The dye tablets will stain your clothes and other fabrics, so wear clothes that you don't mind getting dirty, or wear an apron or smock. Be sure to roll up your sleeves!

TOOLS: Check the "Other Stuff You'll Need" list on page 5. Use jars and utensils that you'll only use for your experiments, not for eating.

GOOD LAB PRACTICES

WASH YOUR HANDS before you start your experiments and after you finish.

NO FOOD OR DRINKS IN THE LAB. You don't want to contaminate your experiments or your snacks!

READ INSTRUCTIONS TWICE. If the instructions tell you to check on your project, plan ahead and make sure you'll be around to keep an eye on things.

LABEL YOUR JARS. Write down the name of your project and the date on a label and stick it to the jar. It's easy to mix up jars, so this will help you keep organized.

KEEP NOTES ON YOUR EXPERIMENTS. Write down your exact steps so that if you want to repeat a project later, you can. Notes also help you remember which ideas worked and which didn't.

CLEAN UP and put away your supplies when you're done experimenting. Wash your used jars and utensils, and seal any open containers (unless the instructions say not to). Wipe down your work surface, too.

YOUR LAB ASSISTANT

Every good scientist has help in the form of a lab assistant (A.K.A. an adult), which is required for these experiments. Your adult assistant will handle all the heavy lifting, like boiling water and carrying around hot jars, so you'll be free to make all the important scientific decisions.

CRYSTAL SCIENCE

Wondering how you'll transform plain old powder into sparkly crystal jewelry? Here's the scoop on the science behind your experiments.

WHAT IS A CRYSTAL?

A crystal is any solid in which the atoms and molecules have arranged themselves into a repeating pattern. The repeating pattern makes the crystal grow in a certain shape. As an example, check out this crystal that you see every day: table salt. A single molecule of table salt is one atom of sodium and one atom of chlorine. When salt molecules arrange themselves into crystals, they naturally form a cube.

TABLE SALT MOLECULE

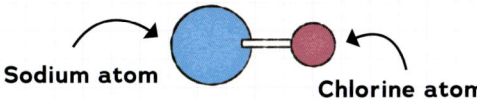

Sodium atom — Chlorine atom

TABLE SALT CRYSTAL

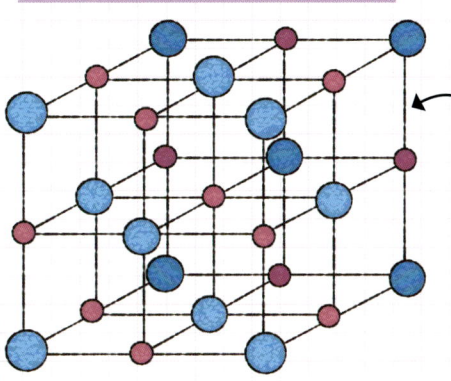

A salt crystal is made of salt molecules bonded together in a cube shape.

Real salt crystals

WHAT'S IN MY CRYSTAL POWDER?

Your crystal powder is made of the chemical aluminum potassium sulfate, also called alum for short. Alum is mined from mineral deposits found in the earth. Along with crystal-making, it has lots of uses, including purifying water. It's also used in pickle recipes to keep things crunchy and as an ingredient in deodorants.

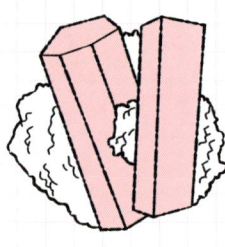

HOW DO MY CRYSTALS GROW?

Before we dive into your jewelry projects, let's take a closer look at what's going on in your crystal-growing experiments. You'll grow crystals in two ways: by using a supersaturated solution and by evaporation. Read on to learn how these methods work.

BY SUPERSATURATED SOLUTION

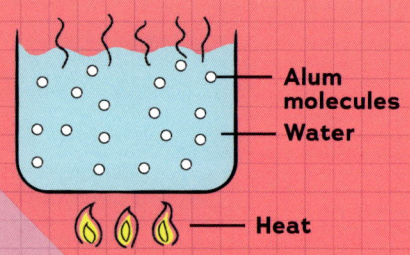

To grow crystals, you'll dissolve alum powder into very hot water to create a liquid growing solution. Heating up the water causes the molecules to move faster and allows more alum molecules into the water. You can mix more alum powder into hot water than you could if the water was at room temperature. This extra alum makes this solution supersaturated.

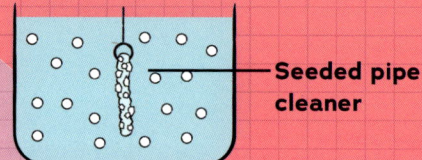

Once the crystal powder is dissolved, the alum molecules float around freely so they can bond together to make crystals. You'll let the growing solution cool a little, and then put in a pipe cleaner shape that you've grown tiny alum crystals on beforehand (page 16).

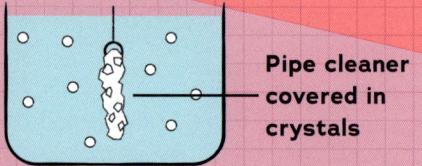

As the growing solution cools, the alum molecules will be attracted to the tiny crystals on your pipe cleaner and will bond to them, making the crystals grow bigger. Eventually the crystals will cover the pipe cleaner.

BY EVAPORATION

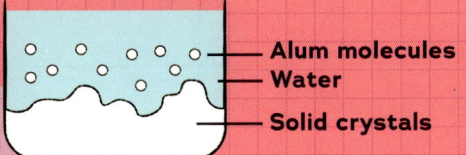

To grow a Colossal Crystal (page 43), you'll use leftover growing solution. At the bottom of your (used) jar, you'll see a layer of solid crystals—this was the extra alum you were able to dissolve into the water when it was very hot. You'll remove these crystals and keep the liquid.

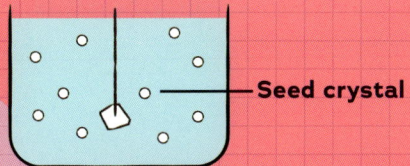

Even though you'll remove the solid alum crystals from the jar, there are still alum molecules in the liquid. This is because room-temperature water can naturally hold a smaller amount of alum. This liquid is called a saturated solution. You'll hang a small seed crystal in the saturated solution and leave the jar open.

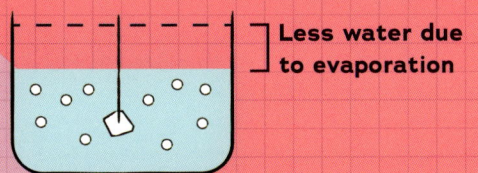

Leaving the jar open lets water slowly evaporate, leaving the dissolved alum molecules behind in the jar. With less water in the jar, this makes the saturated solution turn into a supersaturated solution.

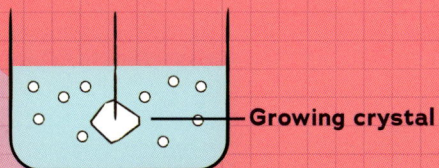

In the supersaturated solution, the extra alum molecules are attracted to the seed crystal in the solution. They attach to the seed crystal and make it grow larger, which eventually makes a giant crystal.

CRYSTALS VS. GEMS

Natural gems can grow a lot like the crystals you'll grow in this book. A gem is a mineral that's considered to be valuable because of its beauty, hardness, and rarity. These minerals form crystals deep inside the layers of rock that wrap around our planet.

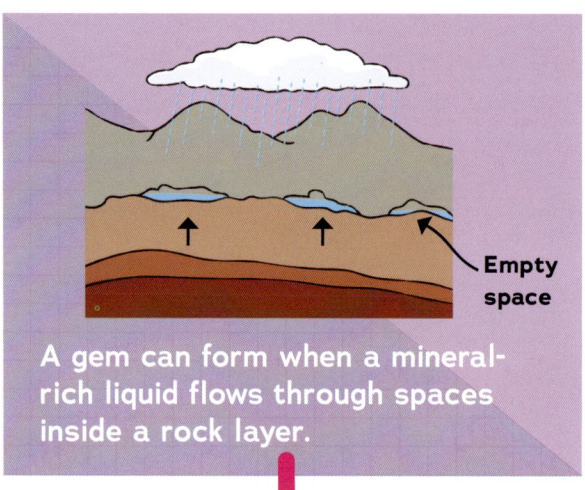

A gem can form when a mineral-rich liquid flows through spaces inside a rock layer.

[Growing gems takes a long time. Diamonds found near the Earth's surface may be at least a billion years old.]

Over time, crystals form as the liquid cools or evaporates. The type of crystal that forms depends on the minerals dissolved into the liquid, the temperature, and the pressure on the crystal. The crystal's size depends on how slowly the liquid cools.

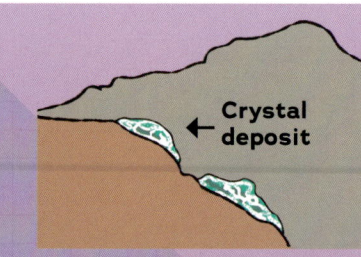

As time passes and mountains are pushed up and eroded away, the crystals reach the Earth's surface. Once the crystals are found, they're mined and removed from the rock layer as rough crystals.

The rough crystal is examined to see how best to show off its inner beauty and size. Once the gem is cut, the surface is polished to perfection and can then be used in jewelry.

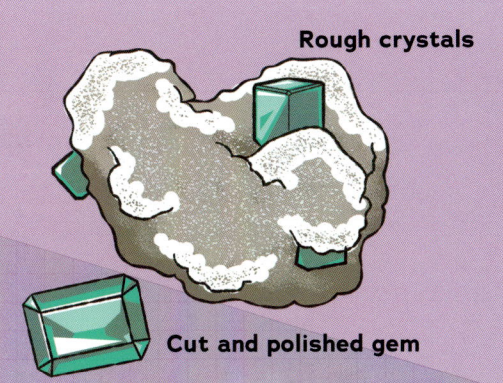

Rough crystals

Cut and polished gem

Mysterious & Magical

People have valued gemstones for centuries. Many ancient cultures believed gemstones and crystals brought their owners good luck or wealth, or helped protect them from harm. Some people today believe certain minerals and crystals have healing powers.

The ancient Egyptians believed that the blue color of lapis lazuli would call supernatural forces to transform their lives.

Not Just Jewelry

Properties of certain gems make them valuable for electronics and other industries. Computer chips are often coated with lab-grown sapphires to help protect them from electric shock.

MAKING SOLUTIONS

You'll need to make two kinds of solution for your crystals. **Seeding solution** forms tiny, microscopic crystals that help jump-start larger crystals. **Growing solution** is what you'll use to grow jewelry and large crystals. Choose your project first (pages 25–46), then flip back here to make the solutions.

What You'll Need

- Masking tape
- Pencil
- Heatproof glass jars with lids
- Measuring spoon
- Crystal powder
- Cooking pot
- Measuring cup
- Distilled water
- Trivet, potholder, and kitchen towel
- Long-handled metal spoon
- Small plastic plate or lid
- An adult assistant

START WITH SEEDING SOLUTION

Seed pipe cleaners the night before you plan to grow your projects. You can even seed several projects ahead of time to get the most out of your solution.

1 Label a small heatproof glass jar with "seeding solution" and the date using masking tape. Add 1 tbsp (15 g) of crystal powder to the jar and place it on a potholder or trivet.

2 Have your adult assistant boil ¼ cup (59 mL) distilled water. Turn off the stove and let it cool for 30 seconds. Then have your assistant pour the hot water into the jar with the powder.

3 Stir the solution with an old spoon until all the powder dissolves. Have your lab assistant put the lid on. Let the jar cool for about 5 minutes so that the solution is still warm, but not hot.

4 Prep your pipe cleaner according to the project instructions. Open the jar and stir the solution. Dip the pipe cleaner in so that it's totally soaked.

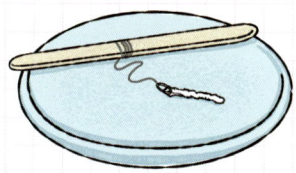

5 Lay your pipe cleaner on a plastic plate or lid. Let it dry completely (overnight is best). Close your seeding solution jar and save it for future projects.

6 After the pipe cleaner is completely dry, tiny crystals should become visible on the fibers. This means the pipe cleaner has been seeded. If not, reheat the seeding solution (page 20) and repeat Steps 4 and 5.

KNOW YOUR H₂O

While the water that comes out of your tap is probably fine for drinking, it may contain minerals that aren't great for crystal growing. Distilled water is purified, so that's why it's recommended for these projects. You can buy distilled water at the grocery store or drugstore—check the label to make sure it says that it's purified by distillation.

GROWING SOLUTION

Growing solution is what you'll use to grow the crystals in your projects. It's best to mix up the solution an hour before you plan to grow your crystals to get the temperature right.

1. Label the jar with your project name and the date. It's best if your jar holds about 10 fl oz (296 mL). Measure 4 tbsp (60 g) of crystal powder into the jar and place it on a potholder or trivet.

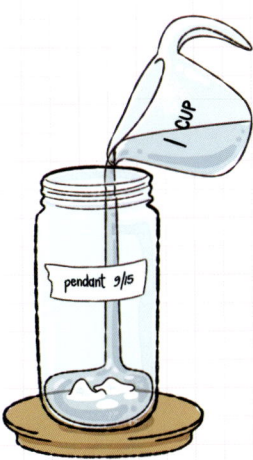

2 Have your adult assistant boil 1 cup (237 mL) of water. Let it stand for 30 seconds, then have your assistant pour the hot water into the jar with the powder.

3 Stir the solution until all the powder dissolves completely. There shouldn't be any powder visible in the solution. If you'd like to add dye (page 21), add it now.

4 Have your assistant put the lid on the jar. Let the jar cool for at least 1 hour. You want the solution to be just a little warm (about 100°F or 38°C) before you grow crystals in it.

TIP: After you're done growing your crystals, keep your leftover solution in a jar with the lid tightly sealed. You can follow the directions on the next page to reuse it for future projects.

If you're having trouble growing crystals, check out page 47 for some troubleshooting tips.

USING LEFTOVER SOLUTION

You can use leftover solution once or twice, depending on the size of the jewels you grow. Plan on using a fresh batch of growing solution with your biggest projects, and use the leftovers for smaller pieces of jewelry. Use up your solution within two weeks of making it, or throw it out.

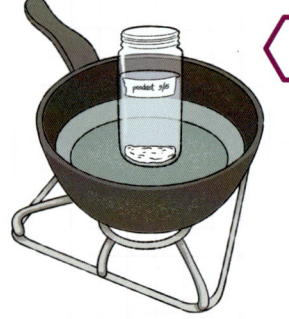

1 Remove the lid from your jar and place it into a pot filled with a few inches of tap water.

2 Your assistant should slowly heat the water in the pot so that it simmers (not boiling) to gently heat the solution in the jar.

3 Have your assistant stir the solution as it heats up. He or she should break up any crystals on the bottom of the jar with the spoon.

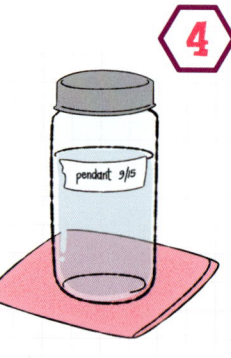

4 Once all the crystals have dissolved, your assistant should remove the jar from the pot and place it on a kitchen towel. Have your assistant place the jar lid on, and let it cool for at least an hour until the jar is just warm (100°F or 38°C).

FILTER LEFTOVER SOLUTION

Dust and dirt in your solution will cause crystals to form randomly (and not on your jewelry). Check to see if your leftover solution is clean, but if not, place a coffee filter over the mouth of a clean jar and put a rubber band over the mouth to secure it. After you've reheated the seeding or growing solution, pour it through the filter to strain out any dust particles.

COLOR NOTES

Your kit comes with four dye tablets to mix up a rainbow of crystal colors. Here's how to get the color you crave.

USING DYE TABLETS

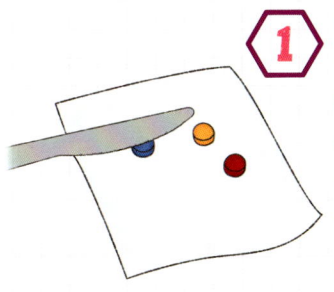

1 Choose the color you want from the chart below and gather the tablets you'll need. If you need to, cut tablets with a butter knife on a piece of paper (to catch the crumbs).

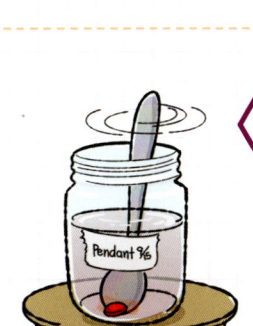

2 Add the tablets to hot growing solution after you've mixed in the powder in Step 3 on page 19.

COLOR RECIPES

CRYSTAL COLOR	DYE TABLETS TO ADD
Pink	1 red
Peach	1 red + 1 yellow
Yellow	1 yellow
Mint	1 yellow + ½ blue
Aqua	1 blue
Purple	1 purple

COLOR TIPS

▶ Glaze colored crystals (page 23) as soon as they're dry to brighten the colors, especially purple. Add two coats of clear nail polish afterwards to prevent the color from fading.

▶ You can use liquid food coloring to color your crystals. About 20–25 drops of food coloring makes a standout shade.

▶ As crystals grow, they try to only attract other alum molecules, so this may make the color uneven. But don't worry! Color streaks make your jewelry one-of-a-kind.

FINISHING YOUR JEWELRY

After you've grown your crystals, add finishing touches to turn your jewels into jewelry.

GLAZING

Seal your crystals with glaze before you wear them. The glaze may make your crystal colors brighter.

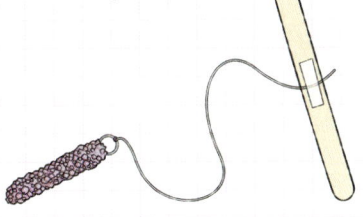

1. Make sure your crystal is completely dry. Keep it on the string and craft stick you used to hang it in the growing solution.

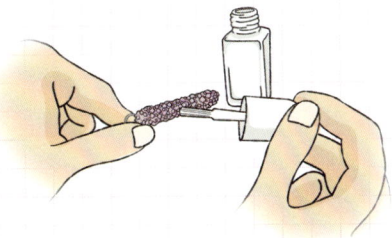

2. Hold the crystal by the string or jump ring. Use the brush to paint a thin coat of glaze onto the crystal.

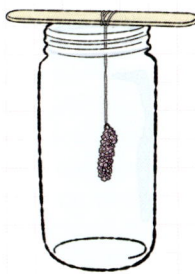

3. Let the glaze dry. If you can, hang the piece in an empty jar to dry. Brush on a second coat of glaze and let it dry.

ADDING JUMP RINGS

Jump rings let you connect your crystals to cords and other jewelry pieces.

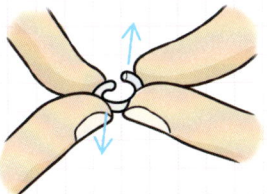

1. To open a jump ring, twist it to create a small opening. Try not to pull the ends apart sideways.

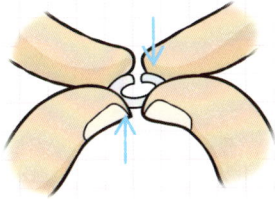

2. To close the ring, twist it back. If you have trouble opening or closing jump rings, ask your lab assistant to use a pair of pliers to help you out.

[**TIP:** For colored crystals, paint on two thin coats of clear nail polish to prevent fading.]

ATTACHING CLASPS

A clasp and cord ends add a classy touch to a necklace.

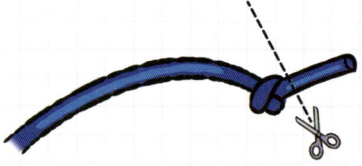

① Cut a piece of cord ½ inch (13 mm) longer than your necklace length. Tie a knot at the end of the cord. Trim off the tail close to the knot.

② Close a clamshell cord end around the knot by pressing the sides together.

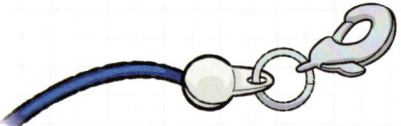

③ Thread a jump ring through both holes in the cord end and the loop in the clasp. Close the jump ring.

④ Repeat Steps 1–3 on the other end of the cord, but attach a jump ring only.

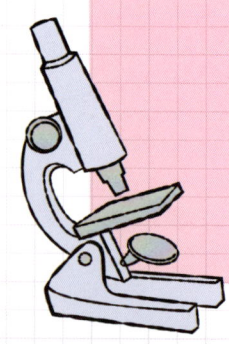

CRYSTALS AREN'T FOREVER

While the glaze coat will keep your crystals shiny, they're still fragile. Try not to drop them or bang your jewelry around. And don't get your crystals wet since they'll dissolve in water.

PROJECTS

CRYSTAL STICK PENDANT

Turn an ordinary pipe cleaner into a chic stick pendant.

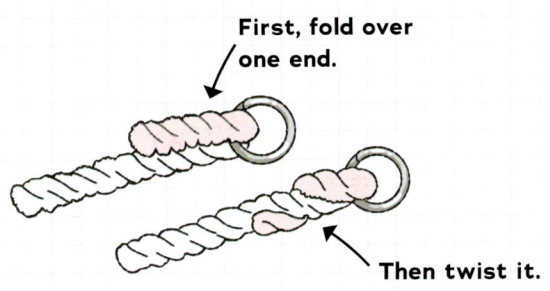

First, fold over one end.

Then twist it.

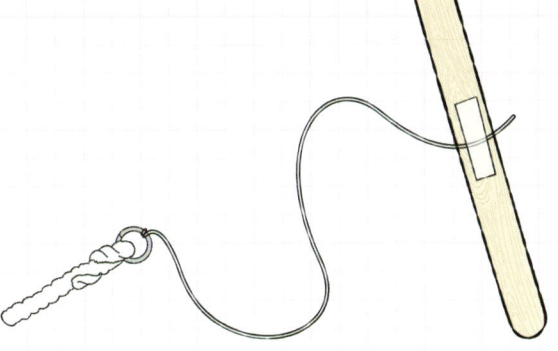

① Cut a 1½-inch (4 cm) piece of pipe cleaner. Fold one end of the pipe cleaner through a jump ring (it's colored pink in these pictures) and twist it once so that it's secure. Shape the pipe cleaner so that it forms a straight line.

② Cut a 6-inch (15 cm) piece of nylon thread. Tie one end to the jump ring and cut the tail of the knot short. Tape the other end of the thread to a craft stick.

What You'll Need

- Pipe cleaner
- Scissors
- 3 jump rings
- Nylon thread
- Tape
- Craft stick
- Seeding solution (page 16)
- Growing solution (page 18)
- Plastic wrap
- Rubber band
- Crystal glaze
- Necklace cord, 2 cord ends, and clasp

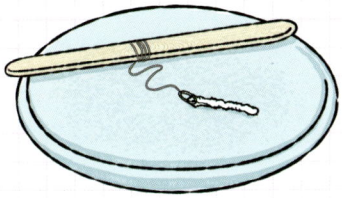

③ Seed the pendant (page 16). Let it dry.

TIP: If crystals start to form on the jump ring, remove the pendant from the solution and clean the crystals off carefully with a needle or a toothpick. It's best to do this while the crystals are still small.

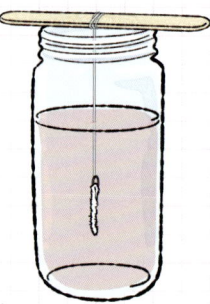
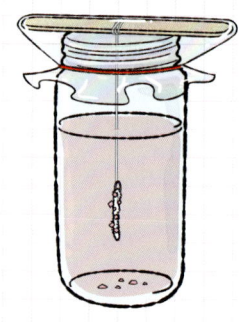

4. Prepare growing solution (page 18). Place the pendant into the solution and put the craft stick across the jar's mouth. Wind the thread around the craft stick so that the pendant hangs in the center of the solution.

5. Cover the jar's mouth with plastic wrap and secure it with a rubber band. Over the next 2–4 hours, crystals will start to form on your pendant. Check on it regularly—try not to bump or move the jar.

6. When the pendant is covered with crystals, remove it from the solution. Hang your pendant in an empty jar to let it dry.

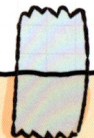

CUT & POLISH

In order to really make a natural gem sparkle, it has to be cut and polished. How a gem is cut depends on its crystal structure. Some gems are cut with *facets*, or angled flat sides that help light bounce around inside the gemstone and deepen its color.

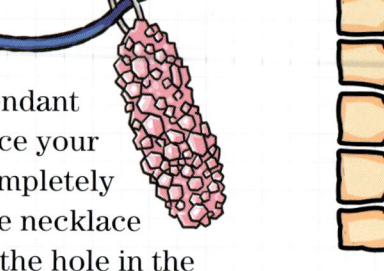

7. Glaze your pendant (page 23). Once your pendant is completely dry, thread the necklace cord through the hole in the jump ring and attach cord ends and a clasp (page 24). Now your pendant is ready to wear!

A cut and polished sapphire

A rough, uncut sapphire crystal

SHAPE SHIFTER

Try making other shapes with pipe cleaners. A bow makes a sweet and simple pendant.

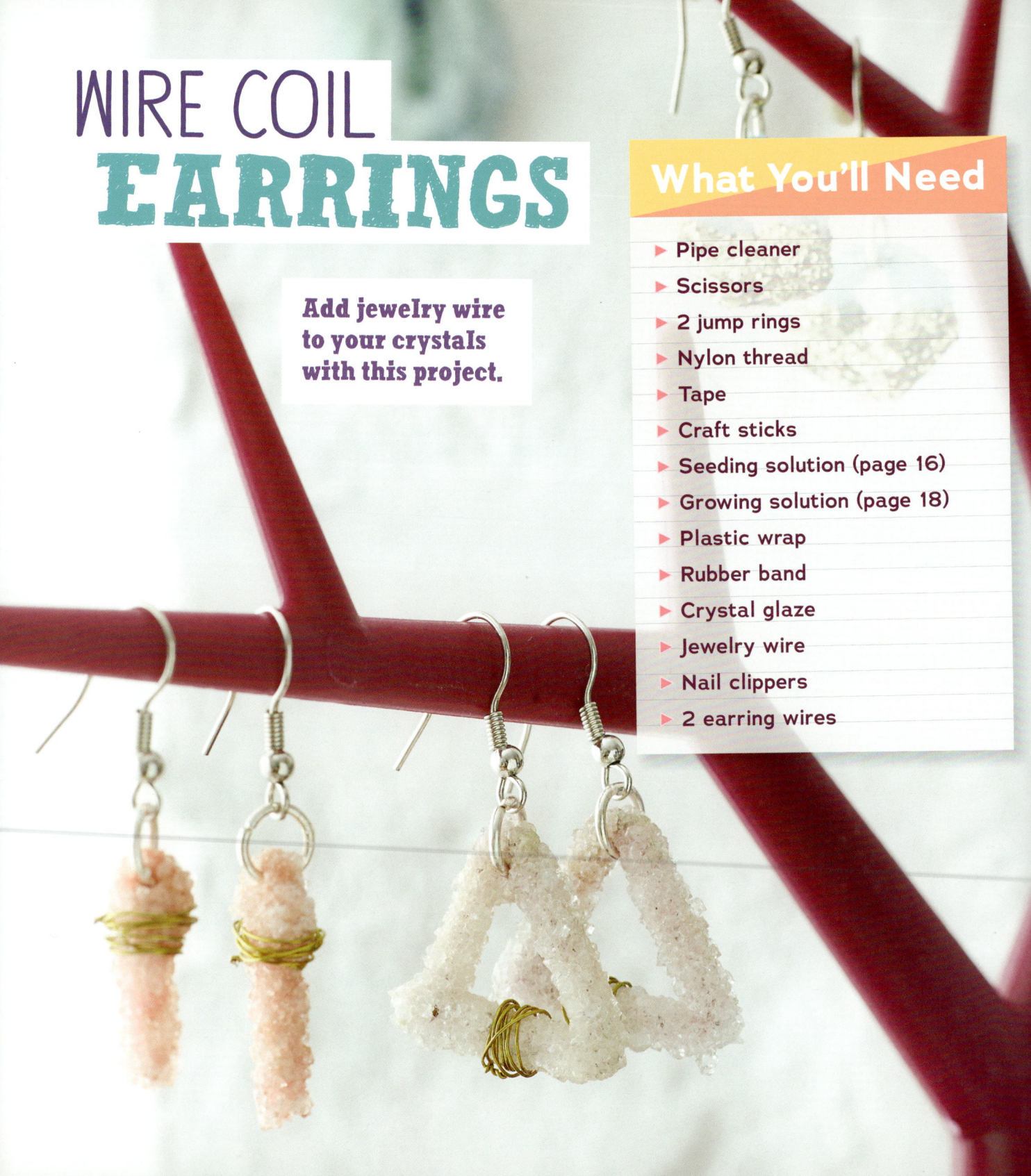

WIRE COIL EARRINGS

Add jewelry wire to your crystals with this project.

What You'll Need

- Pipe cleaner
- Scissors
- 2 jump rings
- Nylon thread
- Tape
- Craft sticks
- Seeding solution (page 16)
- Growing solution (page 18)
- Plastic wrap
- Rubber band
- Crystal glaze
- Jewelry wire
- Nail clippers
- 2 earring wires

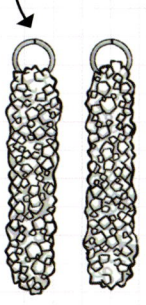
Opening on top

1 Follow the steps on pages 27–28 to make two matching stick pendants. Make sure that the openings of the jump rings are at the top before you grow the crystals. Glaze the pendants and let them dry.

2 Cut a piece of wire 6 inches (15 cm) long. Use nail clippers to cut the wire.

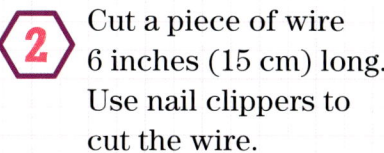

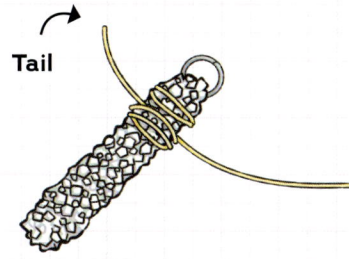
Tail

3 Start wrapping the wire around the top of a pendant, leaving a ½-inch (13 mm) tail sticking out. Gently pull the wire so that it's taut, but be careful not to break the crystals on the pendant.

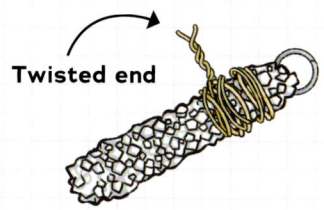
Twisted end

4 Keep wrapping the wire until there's half an inch left. Twist the two ends of the wire together so that the wire is secure.

Tucked-in end

5 Cut the twisted end short with nail clippers. You want to leave about ¼ inch (6 mm) so that it doesn't untwist. Tuck in the end so it doesn't poke out.

TIP: If you want small earrings, cut your pipe cleaners 1 inch (2.5 cm) long before you seed them.

6 Repeat Steps 2–5 with the other pendant. Twist open the jump rings to attach the pendants to the earring wires.

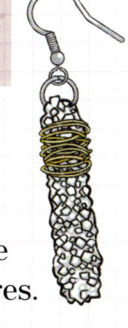

1. Cut six pieces of pipe cleaner 1 inch (2.5 cm) long. Fold each piece in half to make a V shape. (For different designs, see page 35.)

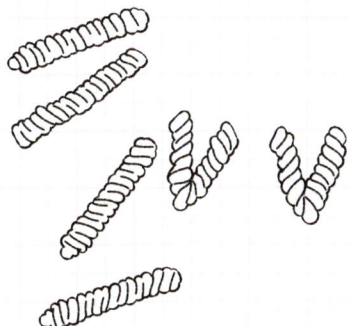

2. Starting in the center, poke two ends of a pipe cleaner into two holes of the ring blank from below. The holes should be next to each other. Pull the ends through so that the pipe cleaner is even.

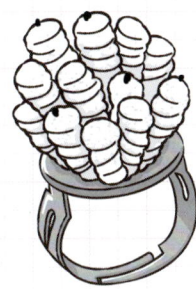

3. Repeat Step 2 until all the holes are filled. Make sure there aren't big gaps between the pipe cleaners—the tips should be close together.

4. Cut an 8-inch (20.5 cm) piece of nylon thread and tie one end around the ring. Tie the other end to a craft stick and tape the knot in place.

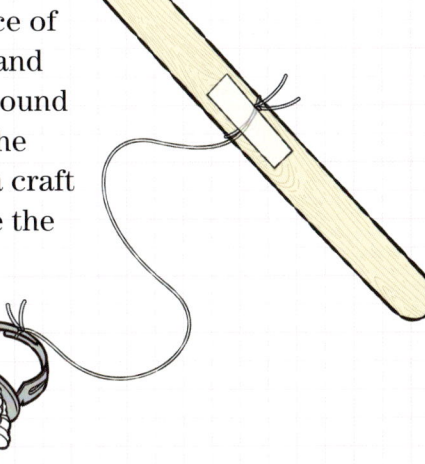

What You'll Need

- Pipe cleaner
- Scissors
- Ring blank
- Nylon thread
- Tape
- Craft stick
- Seeding solution (page 16)
- Growing solution (page 18)
- Plastic wrap
- Rubber band
- Crystal glaze

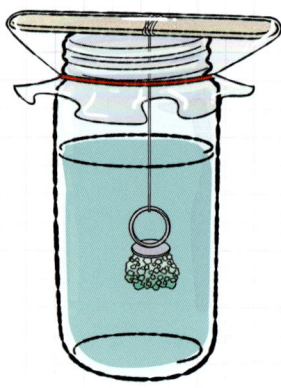
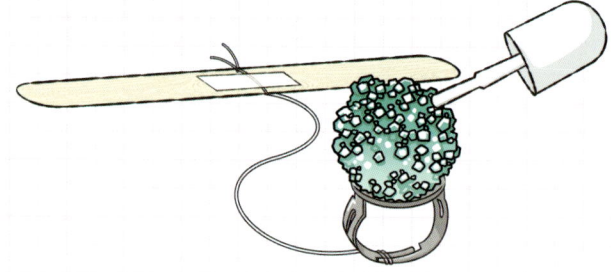

⬢ 5 Seed the ring (page 16) and let it dry. Then follow Steps 4–6 on page 28 to grow crystals on the ring. Remove any crystals that grow on the metal parts of the ring while it's still wet. Then let it dry completely.

⬢ 6 Brush glaze onto the ring. Be sure to get into the spaces and gaps to coat all the crystals with glaze. Let the first coat dry, then paint on a second coat.

CRYSTAL HABITS

The shape of a naturally formed crystal is called its *habit*. There are a lot of factors that affect a crystal's habit, including its chemical makeup and impurities in the crystal. The temperature, pressure, and the amount of space where the crystal grows also affects its habit.

This aquamarine's habit forms long, geometric crystals.

PUT A RING ON IT

Flower ring

Druzy ring

To make a druzy ring, insert the end of a pipe cleaner ¼ inch (6 mm) into a center hole of the ring, from above. Bend the end to attach the pipe cleaner to the ring base. Shape the rest of the pipe cleaner into a flat coil, tucking in the free end.

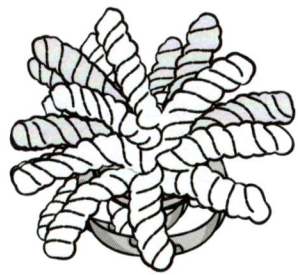

To make a flower ring, follow the directions for the ring on pages 33–34, but cut each pipe cleaner piece 1½ inches (4 cm) long. After you insert the pipe cleaner pieces into the ring, curl each tip around a pencil to create a flower shape.

GEODE SLICE PENDANT

This large, glittery pendant looks like a slice of a real geode.

What You'll Need

- Pipe cleaner
- Scissors
- Nylon thread
- Tape
- Craft stick
- Seeding solution (page 16)
- Growing solution (page 18)
- Plastic wrap
- Rubber band
- Crystal glaze
- Glitter
- Scrap paper
- School glue
- Clear nail polish
- Cord

1 Use a whole pipe cleaner to form a teardrop shape with a hole in the middle. The hole should be at least ⅜ inch (1 cm) wide. Tuck in the ends of the pipe cleaner so that they don't stick out.

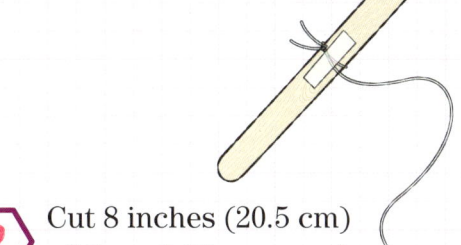

2 Cut 8 inches (20.5 cm) of thread. Tie one end to the top of the pendant. Tie the other end to a craft stick and tape it into place.

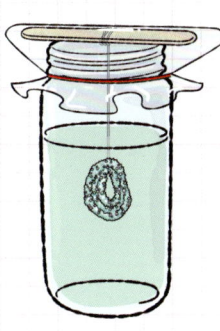

3 Seed the pendant (page 16) and let it dry. Then grow crystals on your pendant by following Steps 4–6 on page 28. Let it dry, then brush on two coats of glaze. If your crystal is dyed, brush on two coats of clear nail polish also.

[**TIP:** Add some bends and kinks to the pipe cleaner to make your pendant look like a natural crystal.]

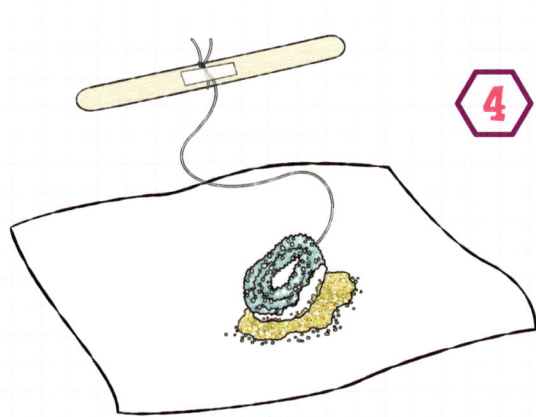

4 After the crystal has dried, pour some glitter onto a piece of paper to make a small pile. Apply glue to the pendant's edges. Dip the edges into the glitter so that it sticks to the glue. Let it dry.

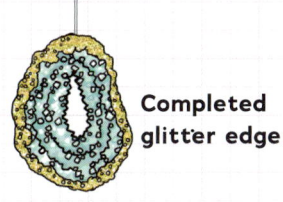

Completed glitter edge

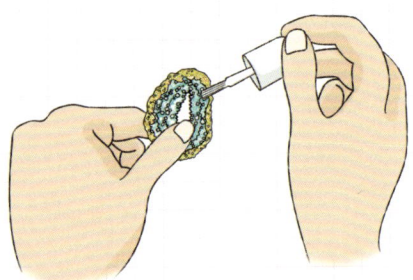
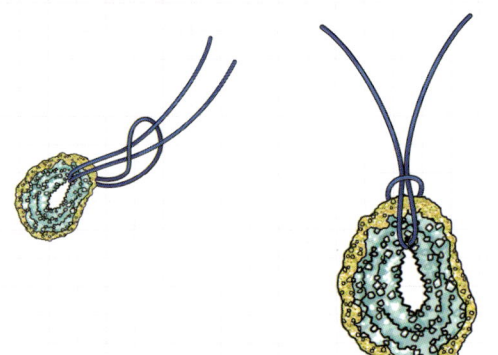

5 Brush clear nail polish over the edges to seal in the glitter.

6 To make a necklace, cut a piece of cord 2 inches (5 cm) longer than you need. Fold the cord in half, and pull the loop through the hole in the pendant. Thread both ends of the cord through the loop, and gently pull them through. Finish the ends of the cord any way you'd like.

A LOAD OF GEODES

Real geodes are hollow rocks filled with crystals. They form when mineral-rich water flows into gas pockets or other empty spaces in a layer of rock. As the water leaks out, tiny crystals form inside the geode from the saturated solution. The crystals may grow larger as liquid flows in and out of the space over a long period of time. Most of the time, geodes have quartz and calcite crystals, but small amounts of minerals such as magnesium or iron can give a geode beautiful colors. Geodes can be small enough to fit in the palm of your hand, or big enough to form caves.

A geode filled with amethysts

A geode cut in half

SHOW YOUR SPARKLE

Try adding a glitter edge to your other pendants, or dip one end of a shape into glitter.

ZIGZAG PENDANT

This pendant gets a color dip to create an ombré effect.

What You'll Need

- Pipe cleaner
- Scissors
- 2 jump rings
- Nylon thread
- Tape
- Craft stick
- Seeding solution (page 16)
- Growing solution (page 18)
- Plastic wrap
- Rubber band
- Growing solution with dye (page 21)
- Cord

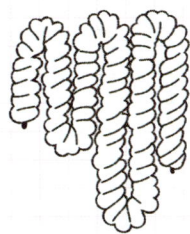

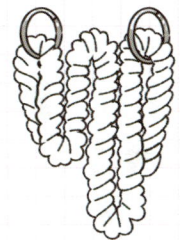

1. Cut a 6-inch (15 cm) piece of pipe cleaner. Bend it into a zigzag shape. Make sure the top edge of the pendant is flat.

2. Thread a jump ring onto each end of the pipe cleaner. Push them along the pipe cleaner so that they sit at the top corners of the pendant. Tuck in the ends of the pipe cleaners so they don't stick out.

[**TIP:** Check the jump rings as your crystal grows—you'll need space to thread a cord through. Use a needle or toothpick to clean any extra crystals off.]

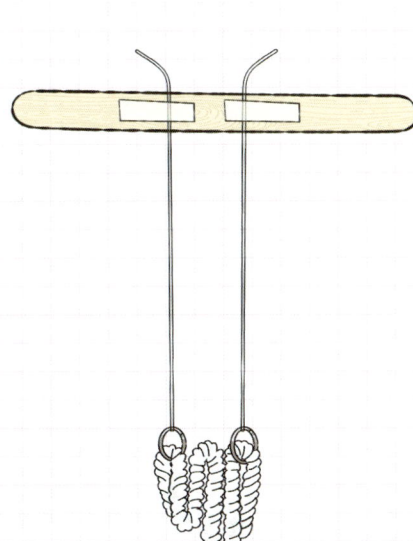

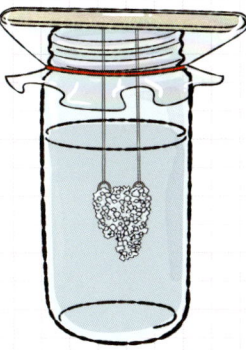

3. Tie a 6-inch piece of nylon thread to each jump ring. Trim the free ends of the threads just enough so they're even. Tape the free ends to one craft stick so that the pendant hangs evenly.

4. Seed the pendant (page 16) and let it dry. Then follow Steps 4–6 on page 28 to seed and grow crystals on your pendant. Let it dry.

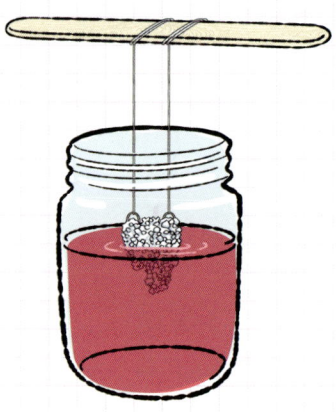
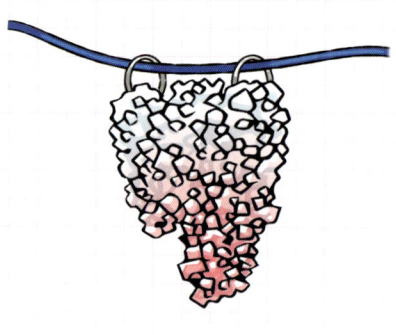

⬡ 5 If you want an ombré pendant, quickly dip the bottom third of your dry pendant into growing solution with dye. The dye will travel up the crystal as it dries, so dip a little first. You can always dip it again if you need to. Remove the crystal and let it dry.

⬡ 6 Glaze the pendant and let it dry. Thread a cord through both jump rings to make a necklace.

Ametrine

Pink and green tourmaline

GEMSTONE COLORS

Pure crystals contain only one kind of molecule or atom, but sometimes other chemicals sneak in when a crystal forms. These impurities can cause the crystal to change color. For example, pure quartz crystals are clear. But if the quartz crystal picks up traces of iron, it may form purple amethyst gems. Or the iron could turn the crystal yellow, and then it becomes citrine. Sometimes you get a mix of amethyst and citrine, which makes ametrine.

COLOSSAL
CRYSTAL

Use your leftover solution to grow a single large crystal. This project takes a bit of extra patience—this crystal took about a month to grow this size.

GROW SEED CRYSTALS

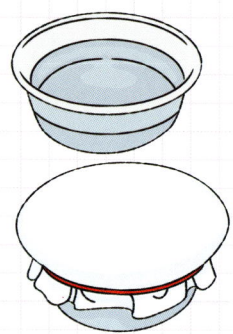

1. Take cold leftover growing solution and pour ¼ cup (59 mL) into a small shallow container. You want at least 1 inch (2.5 cm) of solution at the bottom. Cover the mouth of the container with a coffee filter and a rubber band.

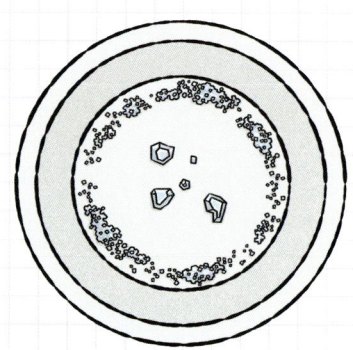

2. Let the solution dry out completely over a couple of days. Try not to bump or move the container, and keep it covered. There should be small crystals growing on the bottom of the container—these are seed crystals.

What You'll Need

- Small, shallow container
- Growing solution
- Coffee filters
- Rubber band
- Paper towel
- Long-handled metal spoon
- Sewing thread
- Scissors
- Tape
- Craft stick
- Crystal glaze

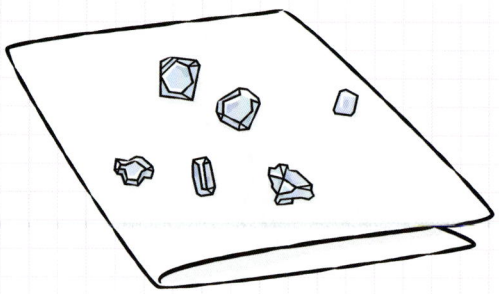

3. Take the seed crystals out and let them dry on a paper towel. Pick the biggest crystal with the most diamond-like shape. It's best if the crystal is at least ¼ inch (6 mm) in size.

PREPARE THE GROWING SOLUTION

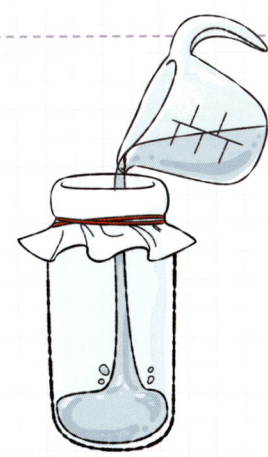

④ Take a jar of leftover solution that's completely cooled. There should be a layer of crystals at the bottom of the jar. Scoop out these crystals and remove them from the solution.

⑤ Filter the solution into a clean jar through a coffee filter (page 20). Cover the jar with a dry upside-down coffee filter for now to keep out dust.

GROW THE MAIN CRYSTAL

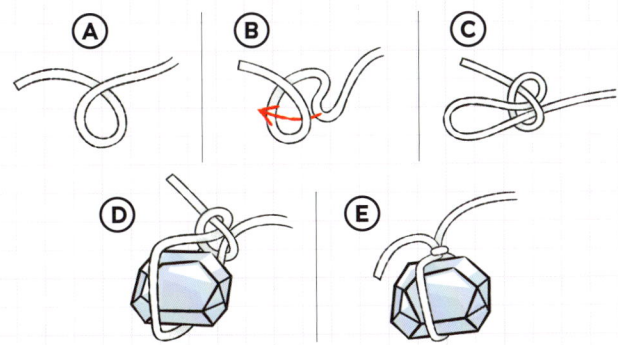

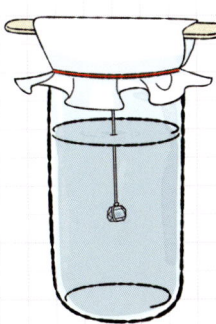

⑥ Cut an 8-inch (20.5 cm) piece of sewing thread. This part is a bit tricky: Take the seed crystal you chose in Step 3 and tie one end of the thread around it. A good method is a slipknot (see above), but any way that works is fine.

⑦ Tape the other end of the thread to a craft stick. Dangle the seed crystal in the filtered solution, and cover the jar with a coffee filter and rubber band.

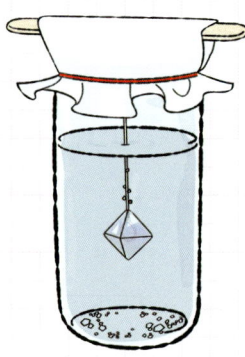

8. Check the jar every day. If tiny crystals start forming on the bottom of the jar, remove the crystal and craft stick and repeat Steps 4–5 to clean the solution. Clean off any crystals that form on the thread, too. Add more filtered solution if you want to keep growing the crystal.

9. Once the crystal has reached the size you want or you run out of solution (it'll eventually evaporate), remove the crystal from the jar and let it dry completely. Brush on a coat of glaze and cut off the thread once the glaze is dry.

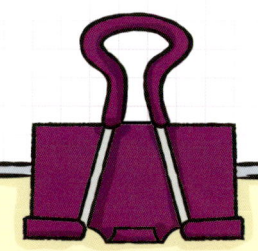

GIANT GEMS

Weighing in at 1.37 pounds (0.62 kg), the Cullinan Diamond is the largest gem-quality diamond ever discovered. It was found in a South African mine in 1905. Since the rough diamond had a flaw in the middle, it was cut into 9 large stones and 96 smaller gemstones. The largest stone, Cullinan I, is a gigantic, 530-carat diamond that's one of the British crown jewels.

Cullinan I

Troubleshooting

Read on for answers to some common crystal-growing problems.

OOPS!

My crystals won't grow.

Here are three things to check:
- Check that you're seeding the pipe cleaners properly. You should see tiny crystals in the fibers. Repeat the seeding if you need to.

- Wait for the growing solution to cool before you put your seeded item inside. If the solution is too hot, then you might accidentally dissolve your seed crystals.

- Still no crystals? Try letting the solution evaporate so that crystals grow slowly, like in the Colossal Crystal project. Follow Steps 4–8 on pages 45–46.

UH-OH.

Crystals are growing on the bottom of the jar—not on my jewelry.

Sometimes dust and other particles can get into your growing jar and cause crystals to grow randomly. Turn to page 20 and follow the instructions for filtering.

YIKES!

My crystal is a giant chunk, not jewelry.

Hmmm, did you forget to check on your crystal while it was growing? Some of the projects in this book are designed to grow quickly, so you really need to keep an eye on things. If you can, scrape off some of the crystals, but you might have to start over.

HMMM...

I don't think I mixed the formula right.

If you think you added too little water: Have your lab assistant follow the instructions as usual. He or she may need to add a little more water if the powder won't dissolve completely. Watch your project as it grows—the crystals may form faster than normal.

If you think you added too much water: No worries, you can still grow crystals, but they'll take a little longer. Unseal your jar and leave a coffee filter or paper napkin on top to keep dust out. As the water evaporates, the solution will become supersaturated, which will make your crystals grow.

CREDITS

Editor: F. S. Kim

Consultant: Troy Blodgett

Cover and box designer: Kristin Carder

Designer: Aruna Goldstein

Technical illustrator: Kat Uno

Photographer: Alexandra Grablewski

Stylist: Amanda Kingloff

Buyer: Kelly Shaffer

Managing editor: Barrie Zipkin

Packaging designer: Owen Keating

Special thanks to: Stacy Lellos, Netta Rabin, Hannah Rogge, April Chorba, Barrie Zipkin, and Armin Bautista

Get creative with more from KLUTZ

LOOKING FOR MORE GOOF-PROOF ACTIVITIES, SNEAK PEEKS, AND GIVEAWAYS? FIND US ONLINE!

 Klutz Books  Klutz Books  Klutz  @KlutzBooks  @KlutzBooks

Klutz.com • thefolks@klutz.com • 1-800-737-4123